To Erik and Heather,

Never give up your dreams –

Bill Day

6/10/93

Day-ja vu

A cartoon collection by Bill Day

Detroit Free Press

DAY-JA VU

Editorial cartoons: Bill Day
Editor: Maria Leonhauser
Assistant editor: Gerald Skora
Project co-ordinator: William R. Diem
Introduction: Barbara Stanton
Library research: Ann Mieczkowski

Published by the Detroit Free Press
Detroit, Michigan 48231

Manufactured in the United States of America

ISBN 0-937247-07-3

Cataloging in Publication Number: 88-71280

To my family and friends
who believed in me
when times were tough

INTRODUCTION

If you don't know Bill Day, you'd probably be surprised to meet him. You might not expect that someone who can put such an edge on his drawings, whose caricatures can be so needle-sharp and unforgiving, can be so gentle and unassuming in person. The cartoons are witty, ironic, poignant, unsparing. The cartoonist is polite, soft-spoken, modest and kind. He is also a rebel and a rabble-rouser.

Look at him, for heaven's sake — lean frame, drooping mustache, faded jeans and good cowboy boots. (He used to wear Hawaiian shirts a lot, but they got too popular.) The style is part outlaw, part country boy, part artist and all genuine. It's the mark of a fellow who knows what he believes, who doesn't mind challenging the established order, and who doesn't tailor his opinions or his wardrobe to the current fashion. That can be pretty subversive stuff.

If you asked Day just what it is that he admires or believes in, he would probably tell you racial equality, social justice, the rights of women, the dreams of children, a world free of brutality and hunger, courage in the face of disappointment, the valor of those who tell unwanted or unpopular truths.

If you asked him what he most dislikes, he would surely say trigger-happy militarists, religious hypocrites, nuclear warheads christened "peacekeepers," sanctimonious fat cats, people who dump on Detroit, promoters of apartheid, elected officials who behave as if the voters are saps.

You don't have to ask him, though. You have only to look at his cartoons.

Some editorial cartoonists depend for their impact on the written punch line. You look at the cartoon, you read the gag line underneath, you look at the cartoon again, you get the point. Bill Day can deliver a funny line with the best of them, but the most memorable Day cartoons don't need explanations: They leap out and sock you right in the eye, the heart and the solar plexus.

When the space shuttle Challenger exploded, Day's drawing of the space shuttle soaring straight into the hands of God said more than any words could. Fifty thousand readers requested reprints of it. After three Detroit fire fighters died in a blazing warehouse, Day drew a Dalmatian with a tear in its eye, a cartoon that touched readers so deeply that the sale of reprints raised more than $40,000 for the fire fighters' families.

Particularly when the subject is civil rights, Day is undisturbed — even delighted — when his cartoons draw blood or set the pack to howling. Yet he has never lost a sense of awe at the power that his talent and his place in the newspaper have given him, and he will spend hours listening, learning and debating earnestly with those who disagree with him.

He is the consummate professional. If Day ever suffers from creative block, his colleagues have never heard about it. As the morning debates of the Free Press editorial board swirl around him, Day roughs out one or two — or sometimes three — sketches on the topics of the day, pausing occasionally to offer an opinion on some issue being discussed.

One of the sketches will be chosen by Day and Free Press Editor Joe Stroud for the next day's paper and turned over the next few hours into a finished cartoon. Week in and week out, the ideas and sketches keep flowing, more than Day could turn into finished cartoons if he worked 10 days a week; there are editorial cartoonists out there who would kill for the contents of his wastebasket.

The possessor of this extraordinary talent grew up in the small town of Lake Mary, Fla., in a household where political discussion was served up every night with the meat and potatoes, and dissent was a family tradition.

As a child, Day watched migrant workers sweating in the fields of central Florida, and the image of those bent-over figures was burned on his mind. Today, the defense of the oppressed and the anger at their condition remains a deep, insistent and eloquent theme in his work.

He is a recipient of four Robert F. Kennedy Journalism Awards, the National Headliner Award, the New York Newspaper Guild's Page One Award, the First Amendment Award, and the Associated Press Managing Editor's Award.

What these honors celebrate is the special power of his pen and brush — the technical mastery, the deep conviction, the fresh and provocative use of familiar symbols, the cartoons that make you laugh and then think, the images that linger in the mind long after the newspaper has been discarded.

Turn these pages. You are about to discover or be reminded of something that thousands of Bill Day's fans and friends already know — that few things are so powerful or capable of moving us as the passion and anger of a gentle man.

Barbara Stanton
Free Press Staff Writer

About the Author

Bill Day, 41, grew up in Lake Mary, Fla. He is the oldest of four children. His father, an aeronautical engineer, and mother, a homemaker, instilled deep political beliefs in their kids at a young age.

The South is very much a part of Bill Day, especially its climate. It is not unusual to see Day sporting shorts and a T-shirt in the middle of a Michigan winter. His home-heating bills are astronomical. But dressing as if he's going to the beach keeps him happy.

His workweek consists of 10-hour days at the office. His weekends are spent at home — mowing the lawn, playing with his three-year-old daughter, Ariel, and palling around with his best friend, his wife, Maria Leonhauser, a reporter for People magazine. He also has a son, William Jr., 22, and a daughter, Emily, 15, from a previous marriage.

Day got his start as a political cartoonist while studying political science and art at the University of Florida. After college, he worked as an illustrator in the art departments of a number of newspapers and did political cartoons part-time. In 1980, the Philadelphia Bulletin hired him as a full-time political cartoonist. After the Bulletin folded in 1982, Day went to the Memphis Commercial Appeal. He came to the Detroit Free Press in 1985.

He does five cartoons a week for the Detroit Free Press and is syndicated by Tribune Media Services. His work appears both in the United States and Europe.

EAST MEETS WEST

June 19, 1987

November 19, 1985

October 14, 1986

December 10, 1987

SUMMIT SOUVENIR PHOTO OPPORTUNITY

December 11, 1987

February 13, 1987

March 3, 1987

SOUTH AFRICA

March 3, 1988

October 7, 1987

August 29, 1986

BillDay
Detroit Free Press
Tribune Media Services
BOTHA'S 'SECURITY BLANKET'

June 15, 1986

January 15, 1986

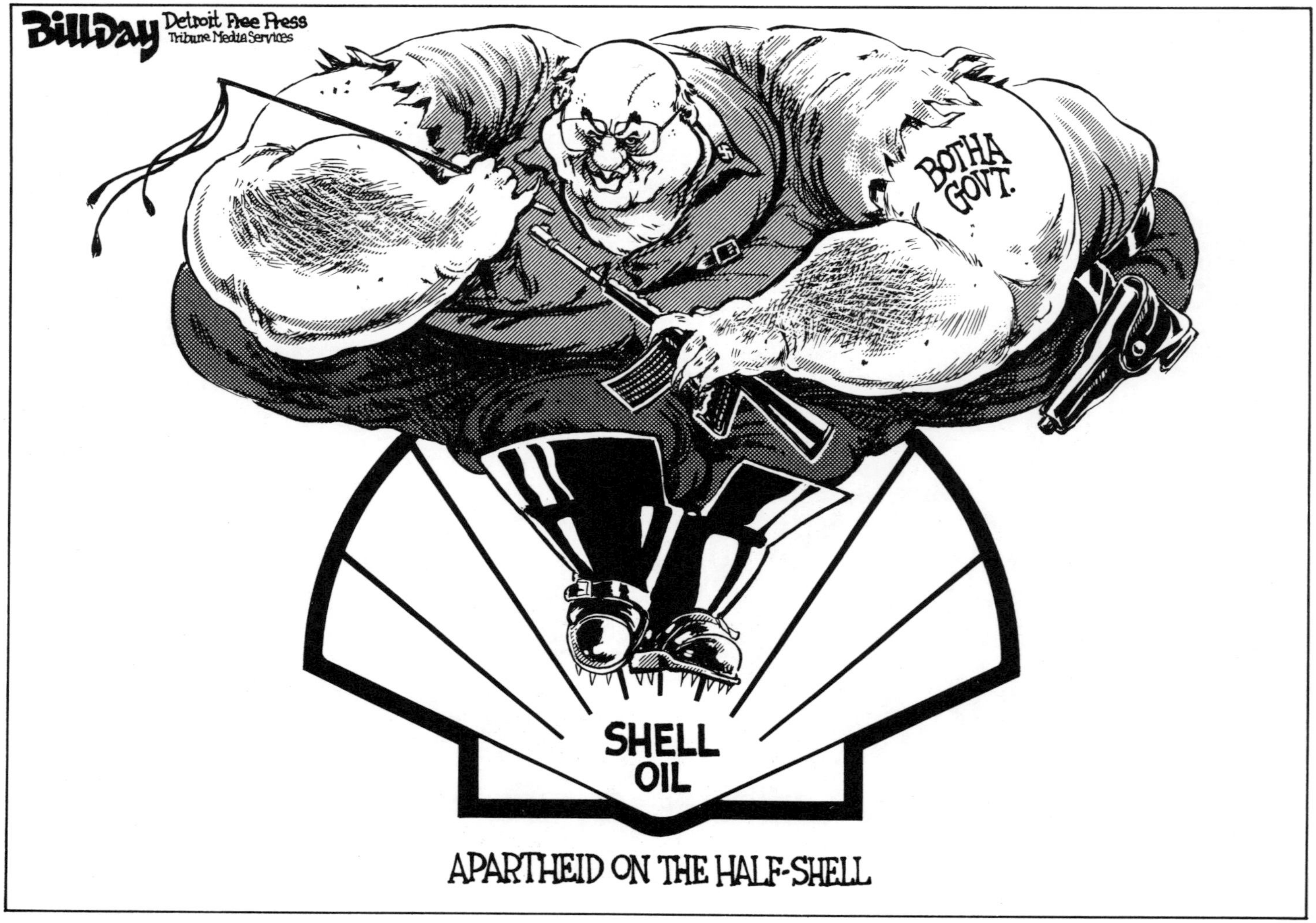
BillDay Detroit Free Press
Tribune Media Services
BOTHA GOVT.
SHELL OIL
APARTHEID ON THE HALF-SHELL

May 16, 1986

October 7, 1986

BillDay
DETROIT FREE PRESS
SOUTH AFRICA
APARTHEID
U.S. CORPORATIONS

May 28, 1985

January 19, 1986

BillDay Detroit Free Press Tribune Media Services
POLAND:
ECONOMIC SANCTIONS!
NICARAGUA:
ECONOMIC SANCTIONS!
LIBYA:
ECONOMIC SANCTIONS!
SOUTH AFRICA:
BUT ECONOMIC SANCTIONS DON'T WORK!

July 3, 1986

BillDay Detroit Free Press
APARTHEID
ALIEN
THIS IS NOT SCIENCE FICTION

July 27, 1986

BillDay DETROIT FREE PRESS
APARTHEID
SOUTH AFRICA
FLAP FLAP SCRAPE SCREECH
SCREECH

July 24, 1985

Bill Day Detroit Free Press Tribune Media Services
I'M A FIRM BELIEVER OF THE 'SULLIVAN PRINCIPLES' IN SOUTH AFRICA.
I'M NOT.
I KNEW IT! ON THE OUTSIDE, YOU PASS YOURSELF OFF AS A CONSERVATIVELY DRESSED, WELL-REASONED PERSON...
...BUT ON THE INSIDE YOU'RE A MAD DOG BLACK RADICAL WHO BELIEVES IN BLOODSHED AND REVOLUTION!
NO... I'M LEON SULLIVAN!

June 5, 1987

THE ADMINISTRATION GRAPPLES WITH ITS SOUTH AFRICAN POLICY:
Detroit Free Press
Tribune Media Services
BillDay

July 16, 1986

December 29, 1987

GLOBAL MADNESS

October 4, 1987

April 20, 1988

October 20, 1987

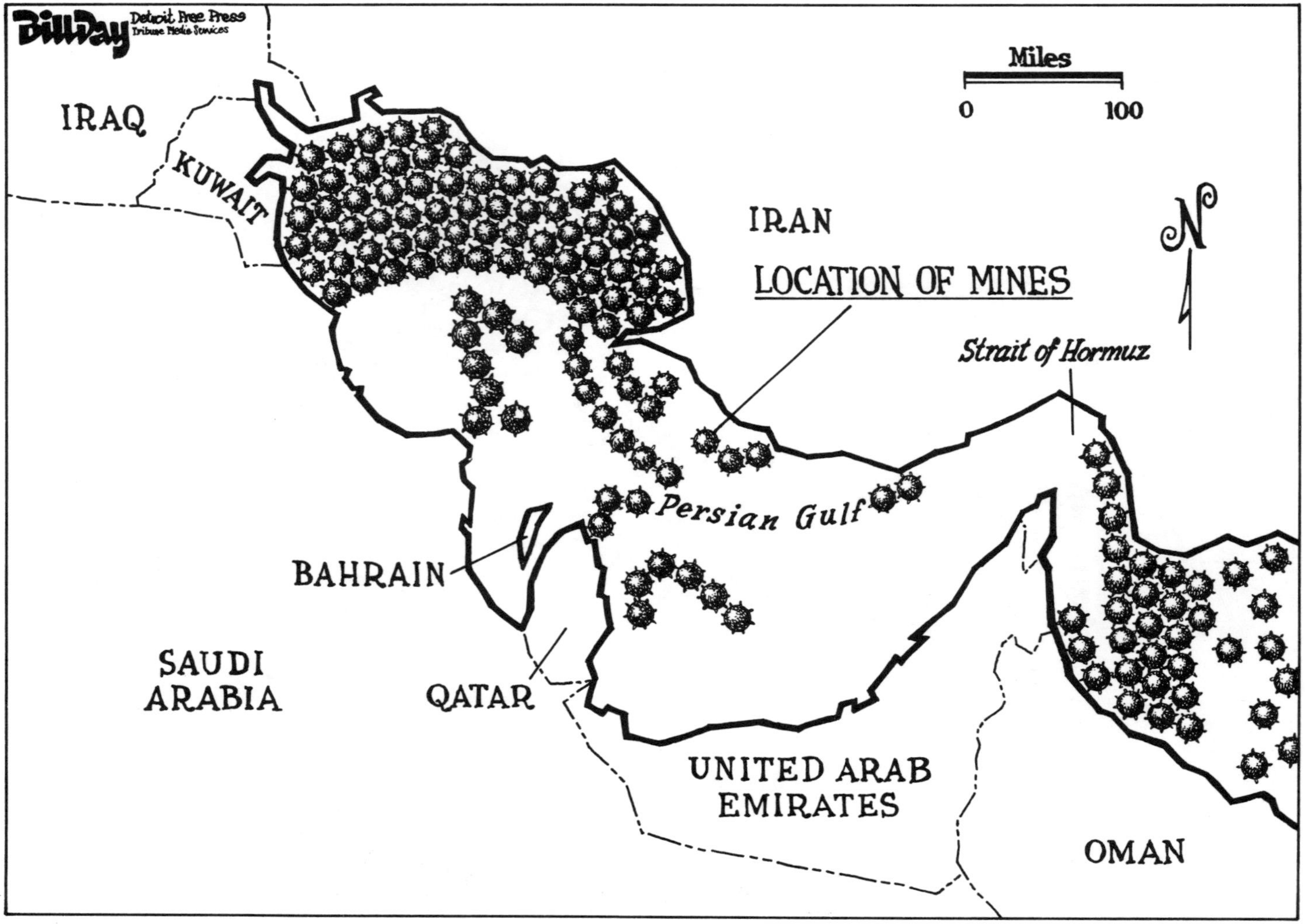

August 12, 1987

July 23, 1987

August 20, 1985

February 19, 1988

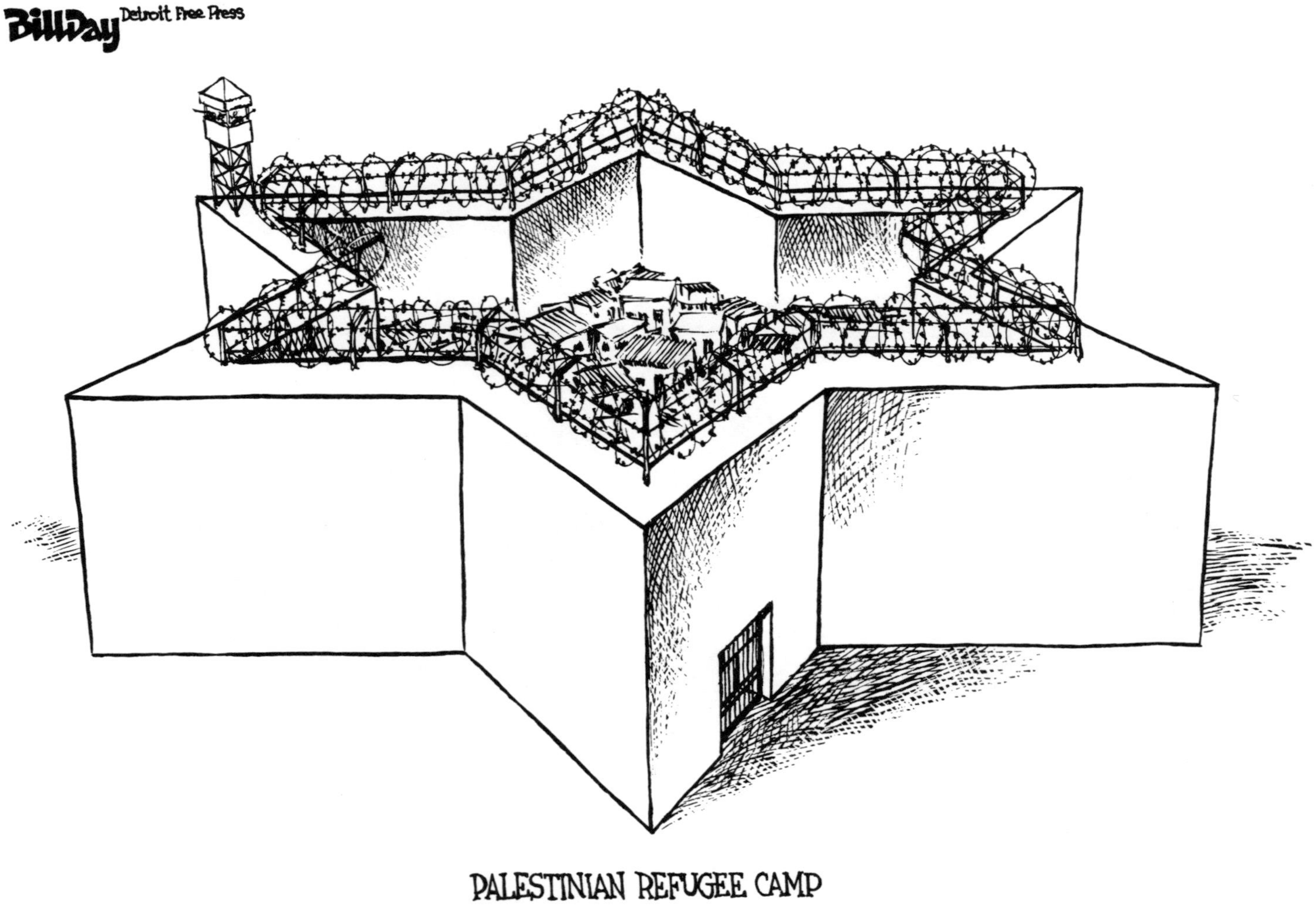

January 4, 1988

DAVID AND GOLIATH (REVISED)

April 13, 1988

December 17, 1986

BillDay
Detroit Free Press
Tribune Media Services
TERRORISM

April 8, 1986

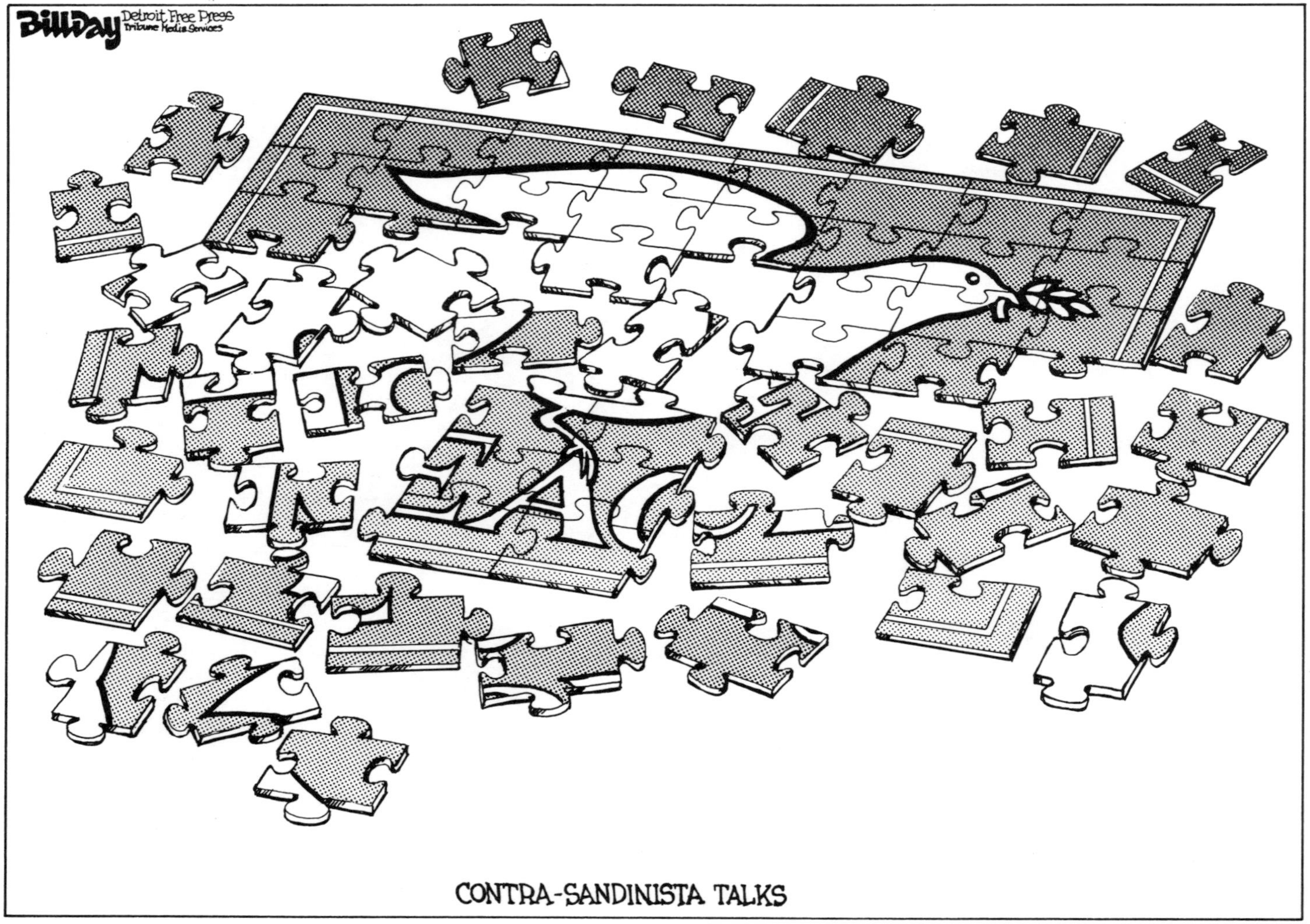

March 24, 1988

October 16, 1987

March 24, 1987

BillDay
Detroit Free Press
Tribune Media Services
YA KNOW, OLLIE, I SURE HATE THOSE NASTY LITTLE SANDINISTAS....
ARF
CHOMP
SNAP
SNIP
SNIP
SNARL
GROWL
SNAP
CHOMP
OH, OLLIE... WHAT HAVE YOU DONE?!
IRAN-CONTRA SCANDAL

July 8, 1987

BillDay
Detroit Free Press
Tribune Media Services
THE BUCK STOPS HERE

July 17, 1987

BillDay
Detroit Free Press
Tribune Media
TOWER
COMMISSION
REPORT
RR

March 1, 1987

January 21, 1988

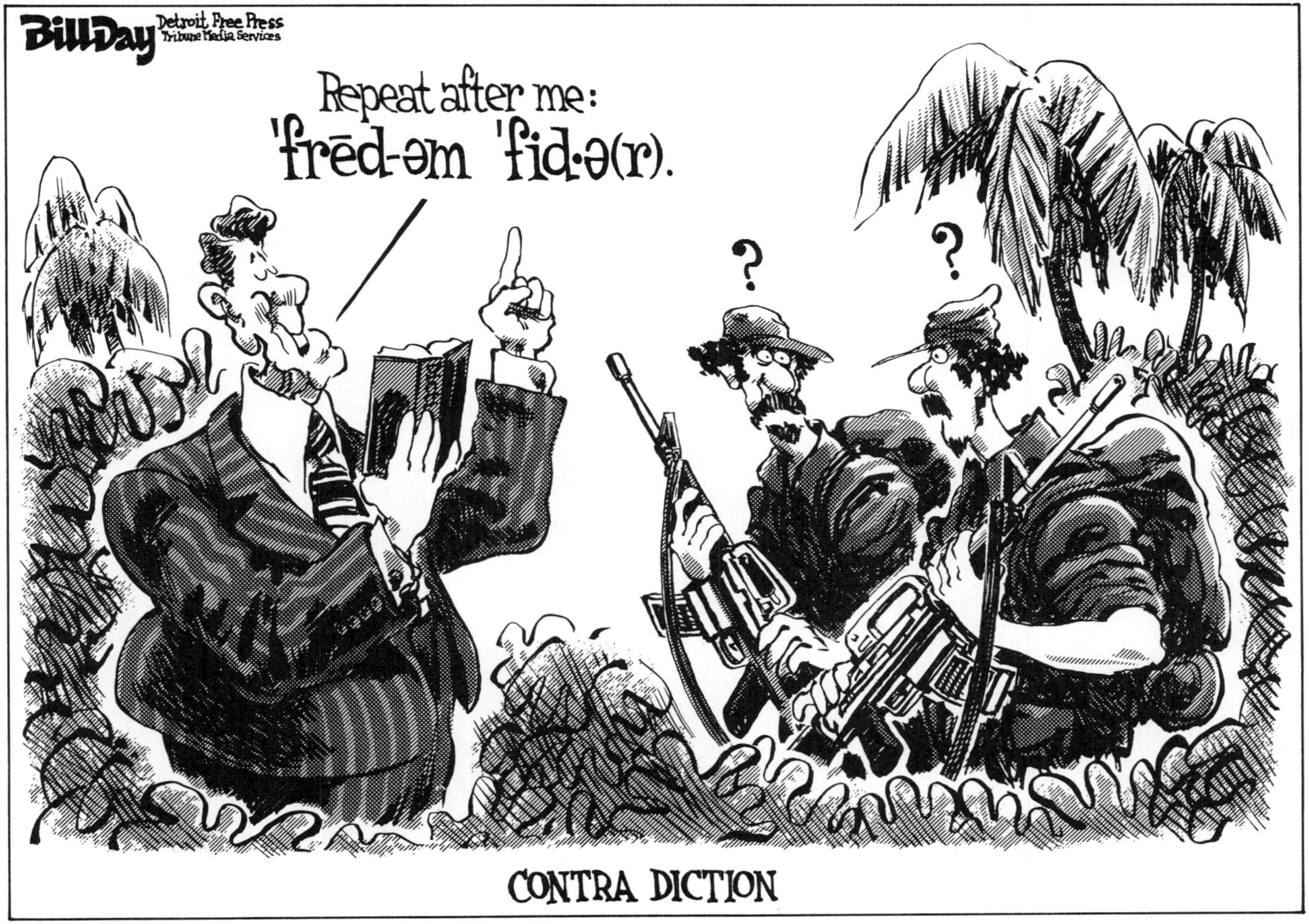

CONTRA DICTION

April 6, 1986

Bill Day
Detroit Free Press
Tribune Media Services
I'M A CONTRA TOO!
I'M A CONTRA TOO!
I'M A CONTRA TOO!
I'M A CONTRA TOO!

June 3, 1986

January 29, 1988

BillDay DETROIT FREE PRESS
REAGAN
The wimps want his Nicaraguan policy to fail. But they made one mistake.
They forgot they were dealing with Ronbo.
RONBO
MORE BLOOD PART II
No Congress, no law, no Sandinista can stop him.

June 11, 1985

April 17, 1986

August 15, 1986

February 21, 1986

October 17, 1986

November 26, 1986

March 20, 1988

August 14, 1987

August 10, 1988

BillDay
Detroit Free Press
Tribune Media Services
AFGHANISTAN
RUGS

May 19, 1988

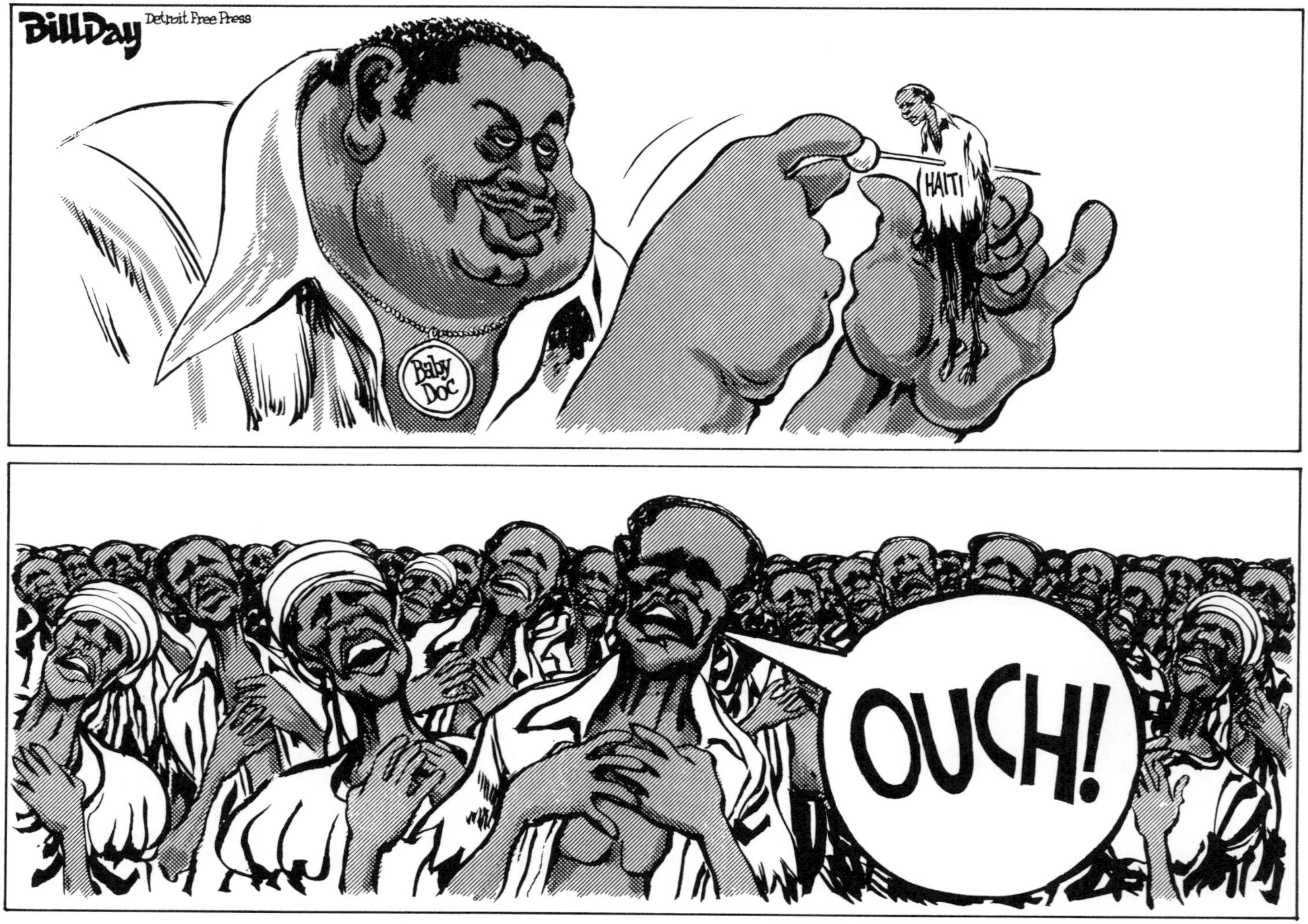

February 4, 1986

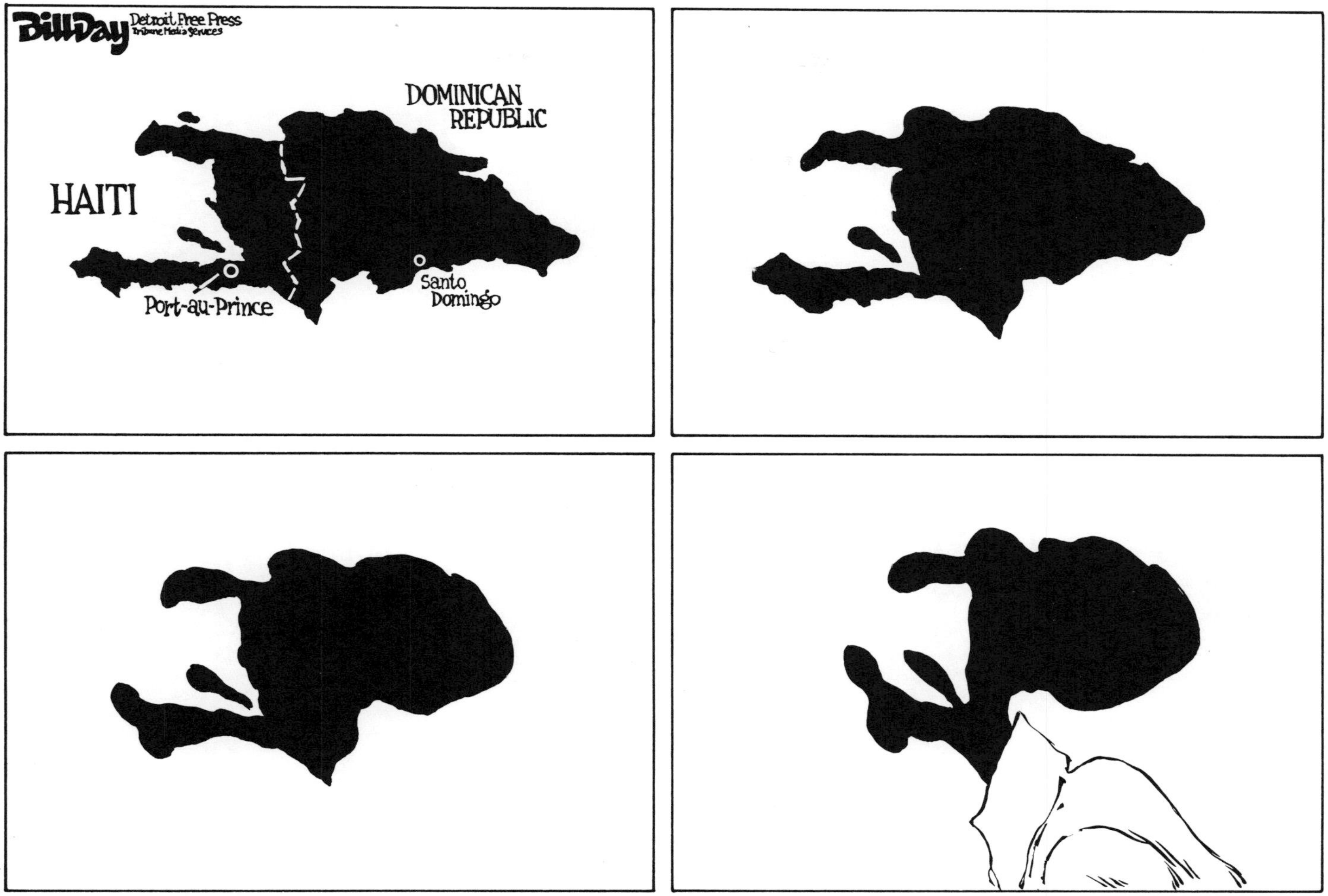

THE SCREAM

January 20, 1988

August 30, 1987

March 22, 1988

October 9, 1987

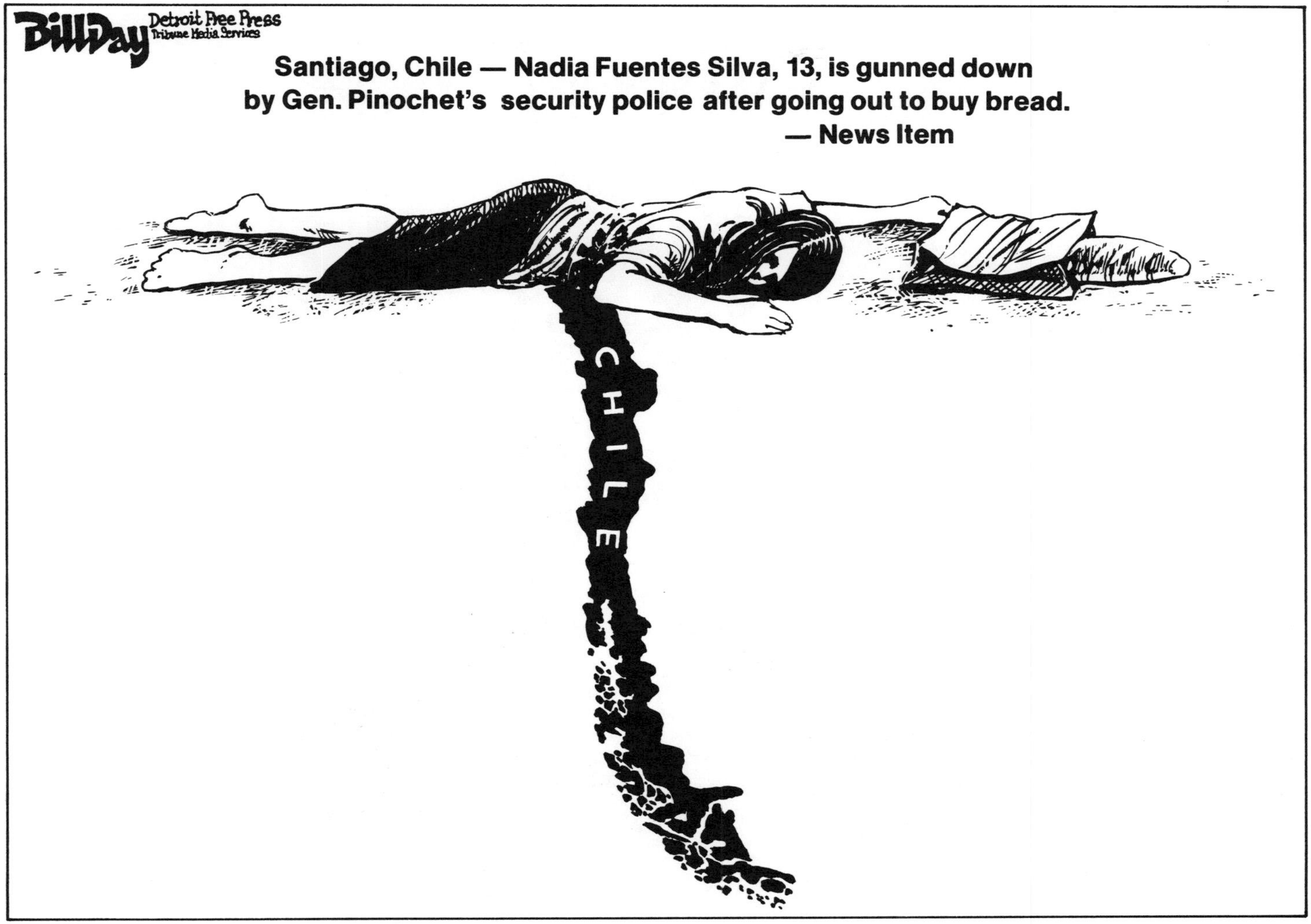
BillDay
Detroit Free Press
Tribune Media Services
Santiago, Chile — Nadia Fuentes Silva, 13, is gunned down by Gen. Pinochet's security police after going out to buy bread.
— News Item
CHILE

July 13, 1986

December 2, 1987

April 28, 1988

SAVE THE HUMANS

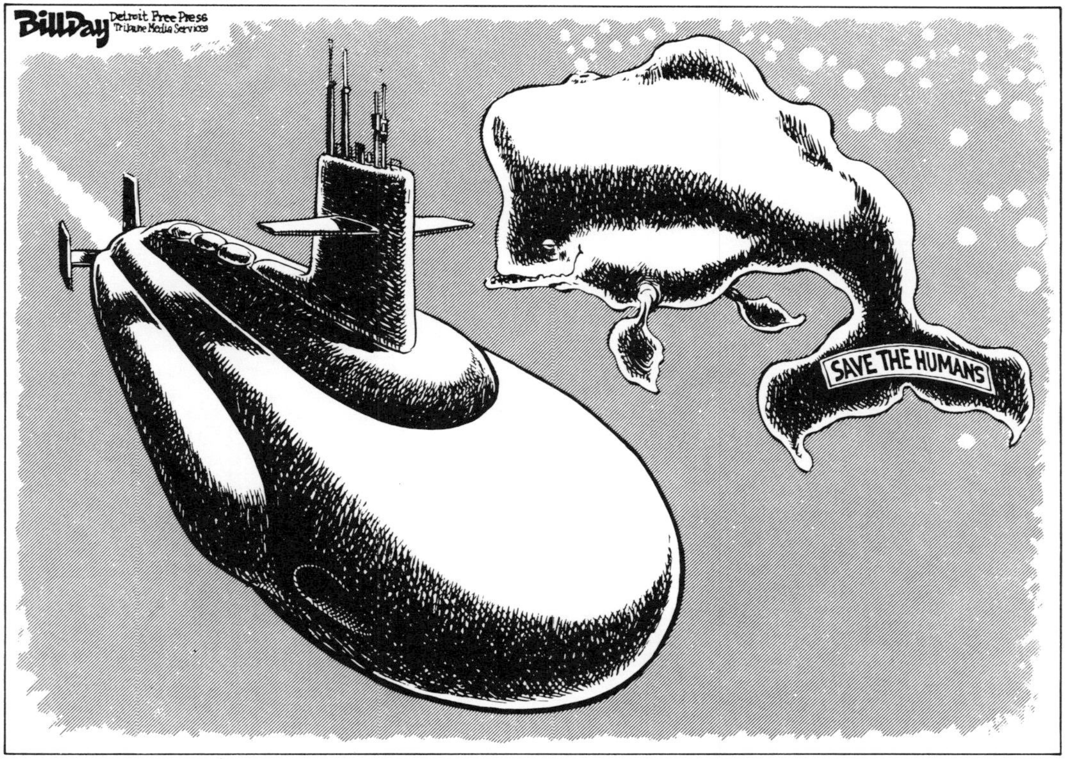

April 13, 1986

May 8, 1986

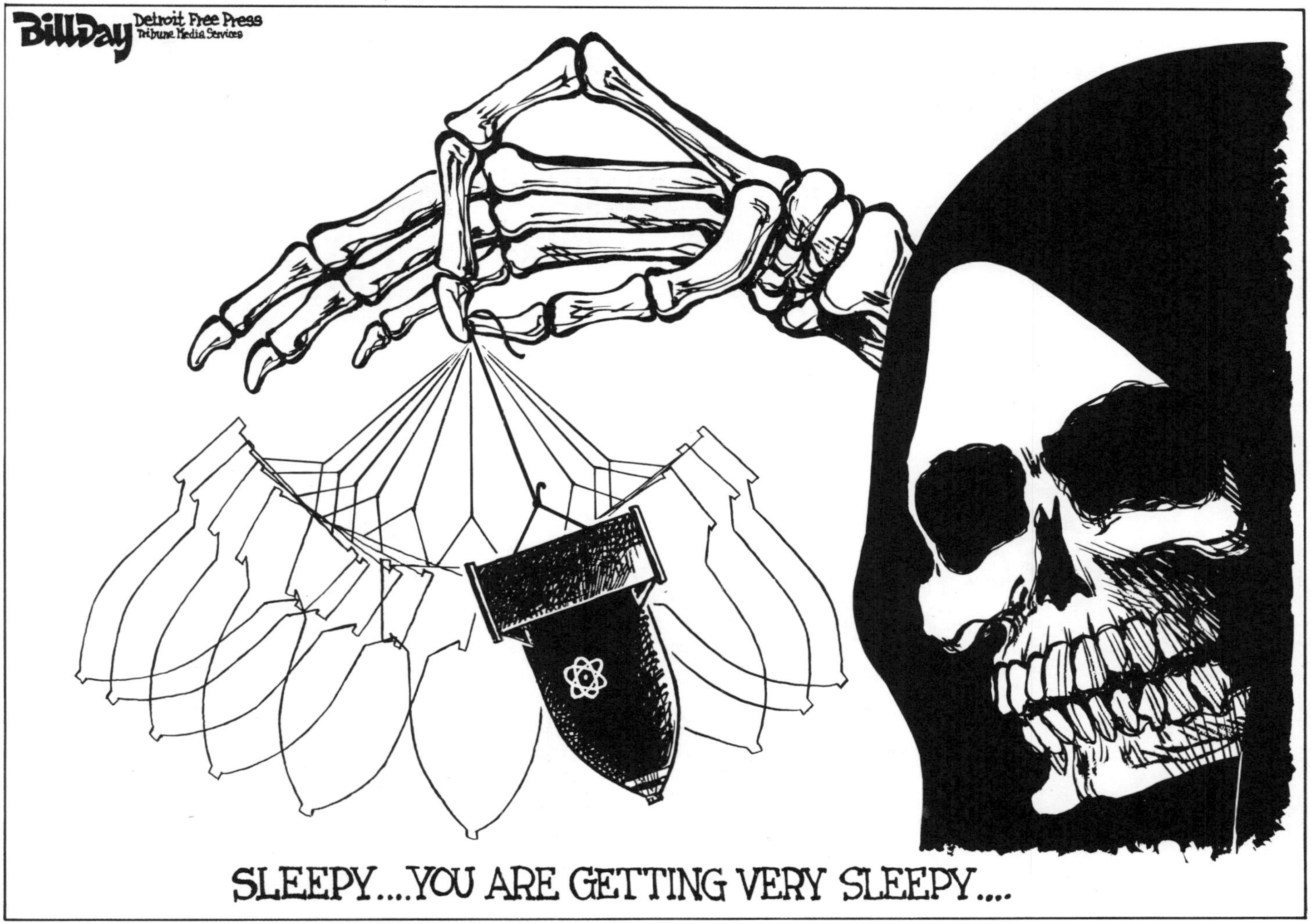

June 24, 1986

December 15, 1987

December 10, 1986

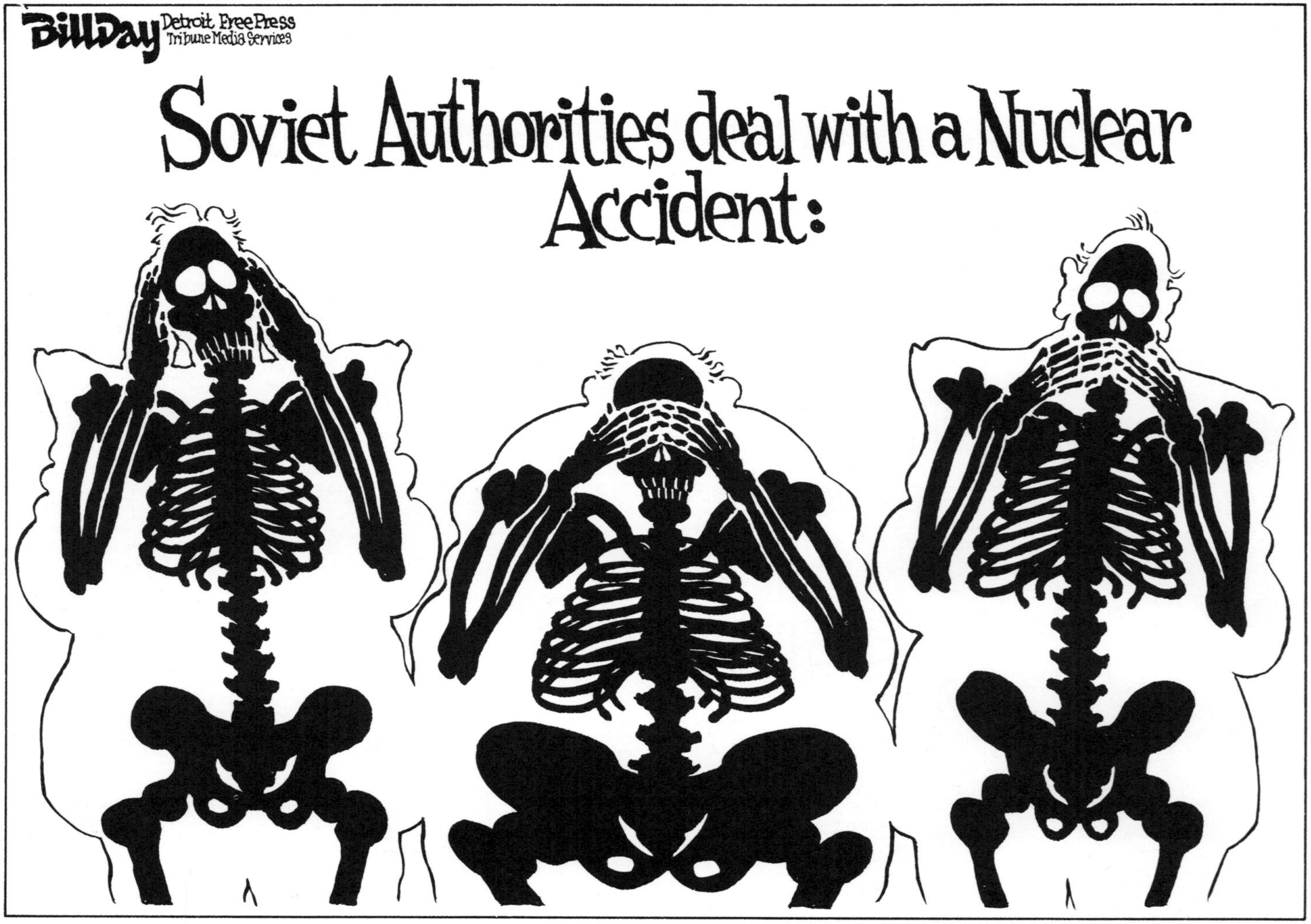
BillDay Detroit Free Press
Tribune Media Services
Soviet Authorities deal with a Nuclear Accident:

May 1, 1986

April 30, 1986

August 11, 1988

BillDay Detroit Free Press
Tribune Media Services
AMERICAN FARMS
THE DROUGHT of '88

June 16, 1988

January 21, 1986

April 10, 1987

October 10, 1986

April 22, 1987

HUNGER

November 27, 1986

November 19, 1987

BillDay
Detroit Free Press
Tribune Media Services
REAGAN: PEOPLE HUNGRY BECAUSE THEY DON'T KNOW WHERE TO LOOK
NOPE, NOTHING IN THIS ONE....

May 25, 1986

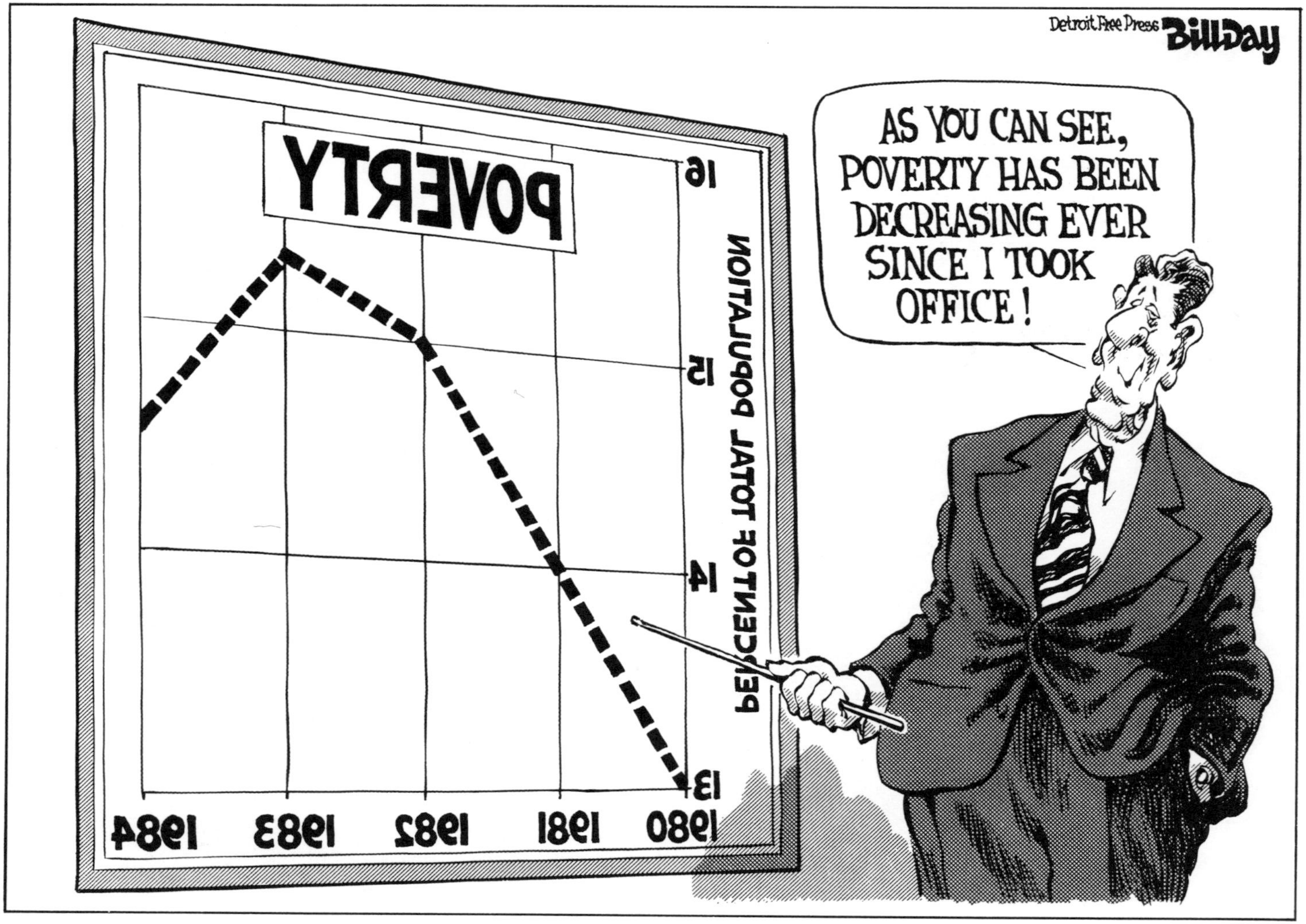

August 29, 1985

BillDay Detroit Free Press Tribune Media Services
CAKE, ANYONE ?
REAGAN TO POOR: GO TO WHERE THE FOOD IS!

May 5, 1986

January 10, 1988

December 18, 1986

February 28, 1986

November 14, 1985

November 16, 1986

November 28, 1985

GIMME THAT OLD TIME RELIGION

July 11, 1985

BillDay DETROIT FREE PRESS
LET US HAVE A MOMENT OF SILENCE...
STATE
CHURCH
ZAP!
SUPREME COURT
DECISION
BOOM!

June 6, 1985

October 29, 1986

August 21, 1985

May 29, 1987

December 6, 1985

April 28, 1987

August 20, 1986

September 29, 1985

LET FREEDOM RING

November 12, 1985

August 2, 1987

Bill Day Detroit Free Press Tribune Media Services
....HOW AH LOVE YA, HOW AH LOVE YA...
CIVIL RIGHTS
RON DOES HIS AL JOLSON IMITATION

June 4, 1986

March 18, 1988

March 30, 1986

Bill Day
Detroit Free Press
Tribune Media Services
GO BACK TO AFRICA!
GO BACK TO ISRAEL!
GO BACK TO EUROPE!

July 17, 1986

January 18, 1987

September 25, 1987

September 22, 1987

April 29, 1986

February 12, 1987

November 7, 1986

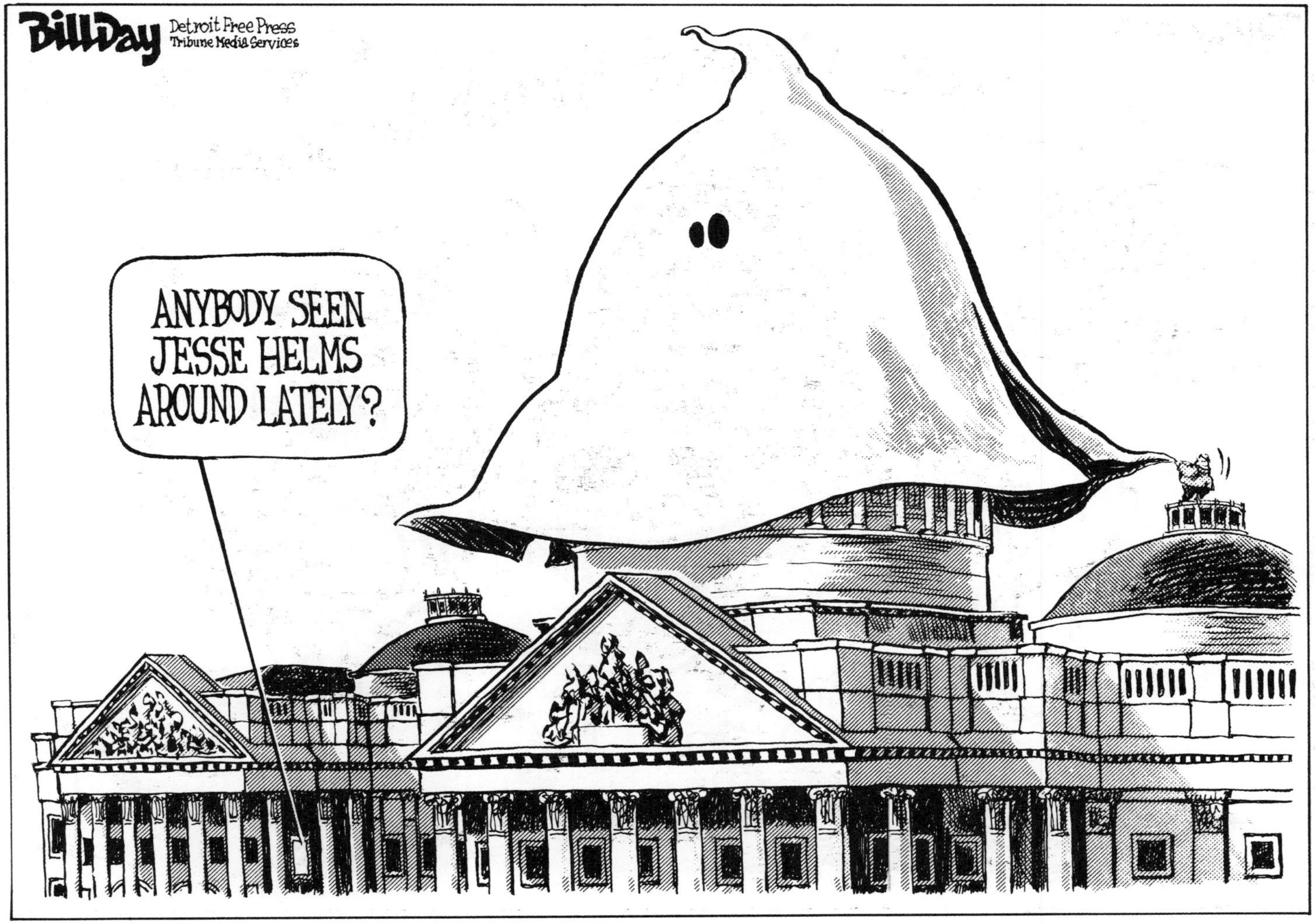

August 2, 1985

August 25, 1988

October 8, 1985

BillDay Detroit Free Press Tribune Media Services
JUSTICE
JUST US
MEESE

July 2, 1987

April 27, 1988

BillDay Detroit Free Press Tribune Media Services
SANCTUARY MOVEMENT
"GIVE ME YOUR RICH, YOUR FAMOUS, YOUR RULING CLASSES..."

May 29, 1986

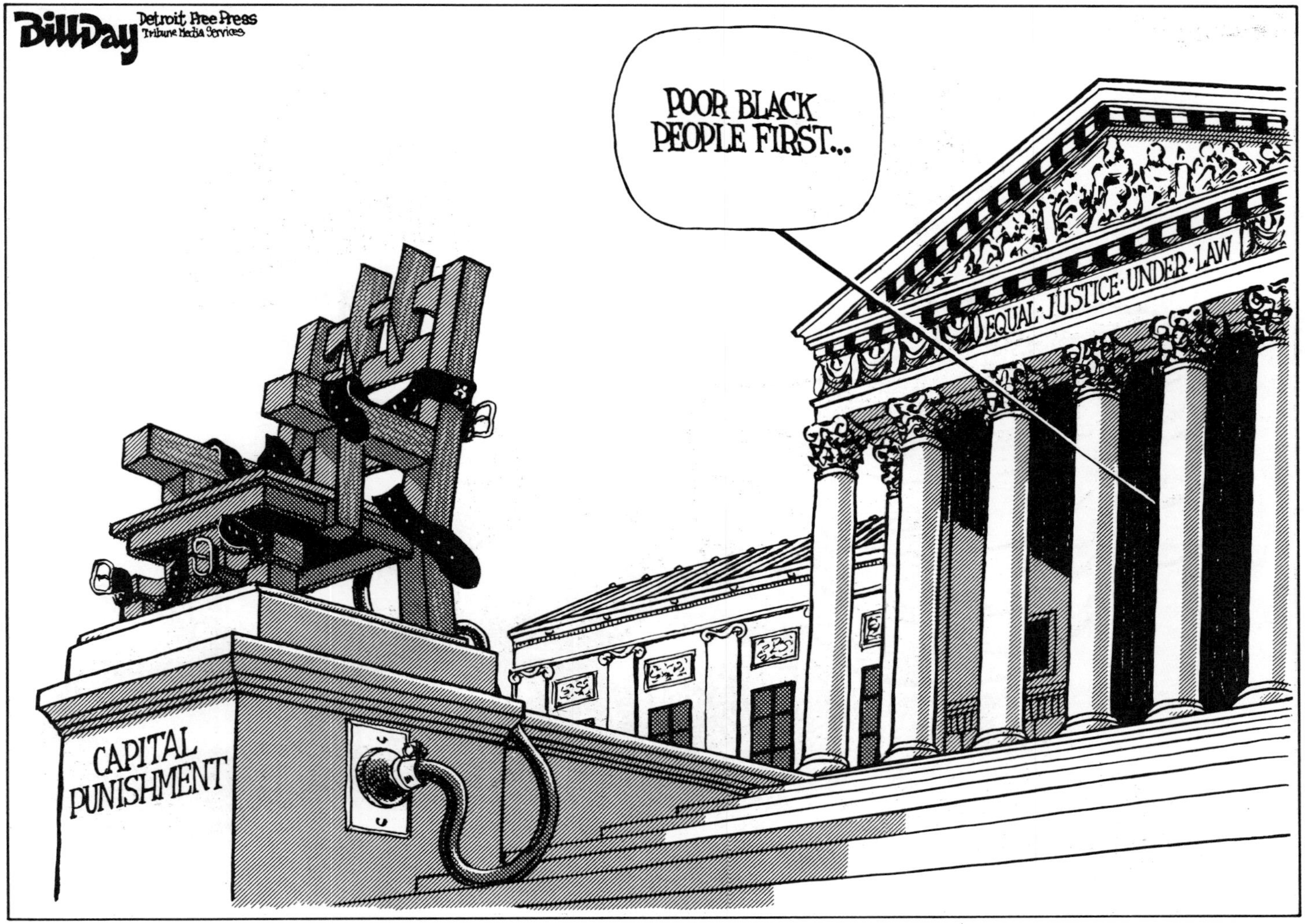

April 24, 1987

November 4, 1987

September 17, 1987

BillDay
Detroit Free Press
Tribune Media Services
NA-NU
NA-NU
Bork
from
the right-
wing planet
Ork

July 7, 1987

BillDay
Detroit Free Press
Tribune Media Services
REHNQUIST
CIVIL RIGHTS

July 31, 1986

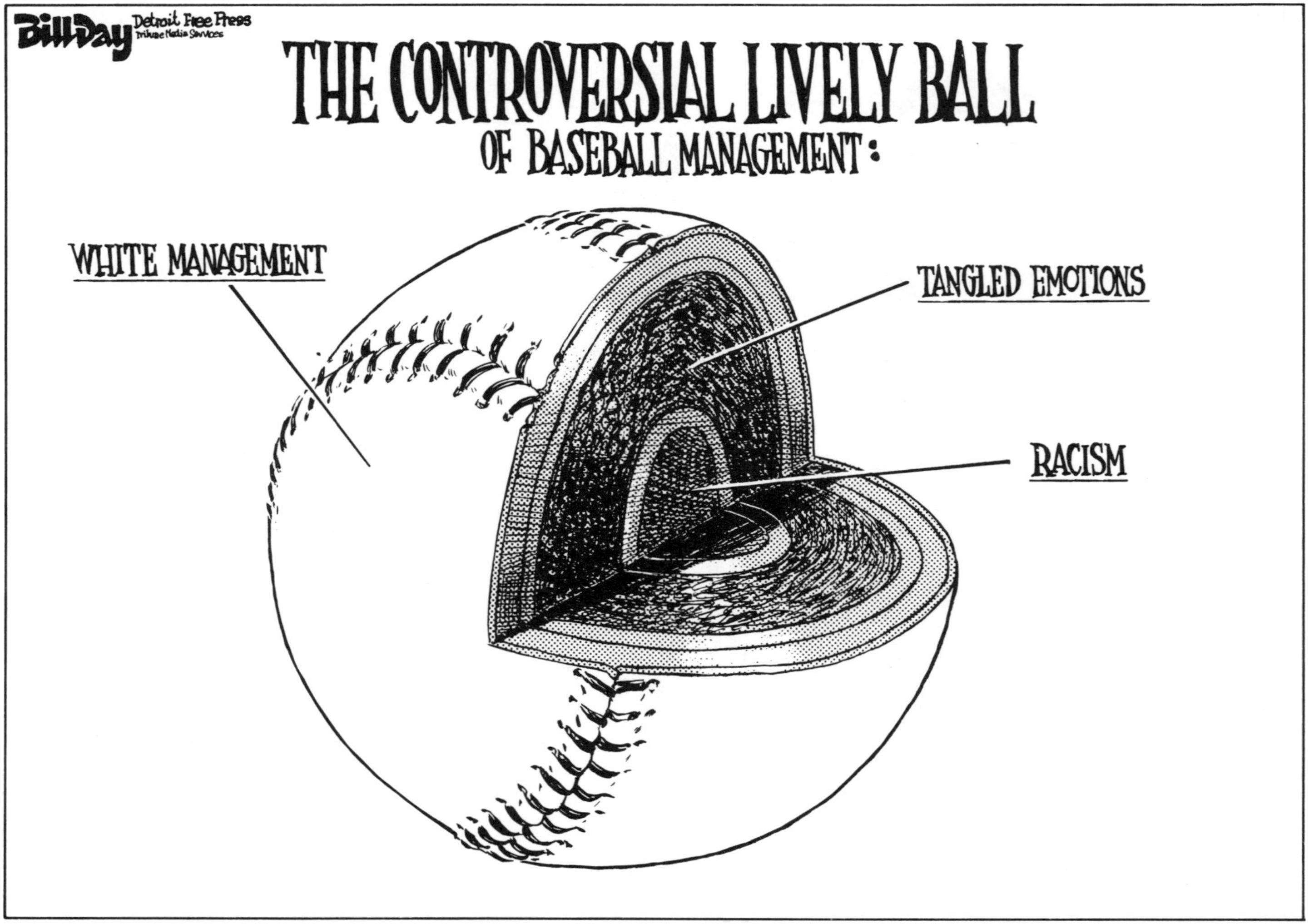
Bill Day Detroit Free Press Tribune Media Services
THE CONTROVERSIAL LIVELY BALL
OF BASEBALL MANAGEMENT:
WHITE MANAGEMENT
TANGLED EMOTIONS
RACISM

June 17, 1987

BILL DAY Detroit Free Press Tribune Media
... I SAID I HATE YOU 'CAUSE YOU LOOK DIFFERENT!!

March 8, 1987

November 7, 1985

BillDay
Detroit Free Press
Tribune Media Services
The 'American Woman'
By Don Regan
HAIR BY MR. JULIUS
UNDERSIZED FEMALE BRAIN DOESN'T UNDERSTAND COMPLEX ISSUES LIKE NUCLEAR 'THROW-WEIGHTS'
NOSE BY A 'FAMOUS COSMETIC SURGEON'
FACE BY ELIZABETH ARDEN
BRONZE TAN FROM EXCLUSIVE TENNIS CLUB
EXPENSIVE DIAMOND JEWELRY MINED IN S. AFRICA
PURSE BY HERMÈS CONTAINING HUSBAND'S GOLD CARDS
DRESS BY OSCAR de la RENTA
SOUTH AFRICAN CHROMIUM STAND

July 20, 1986

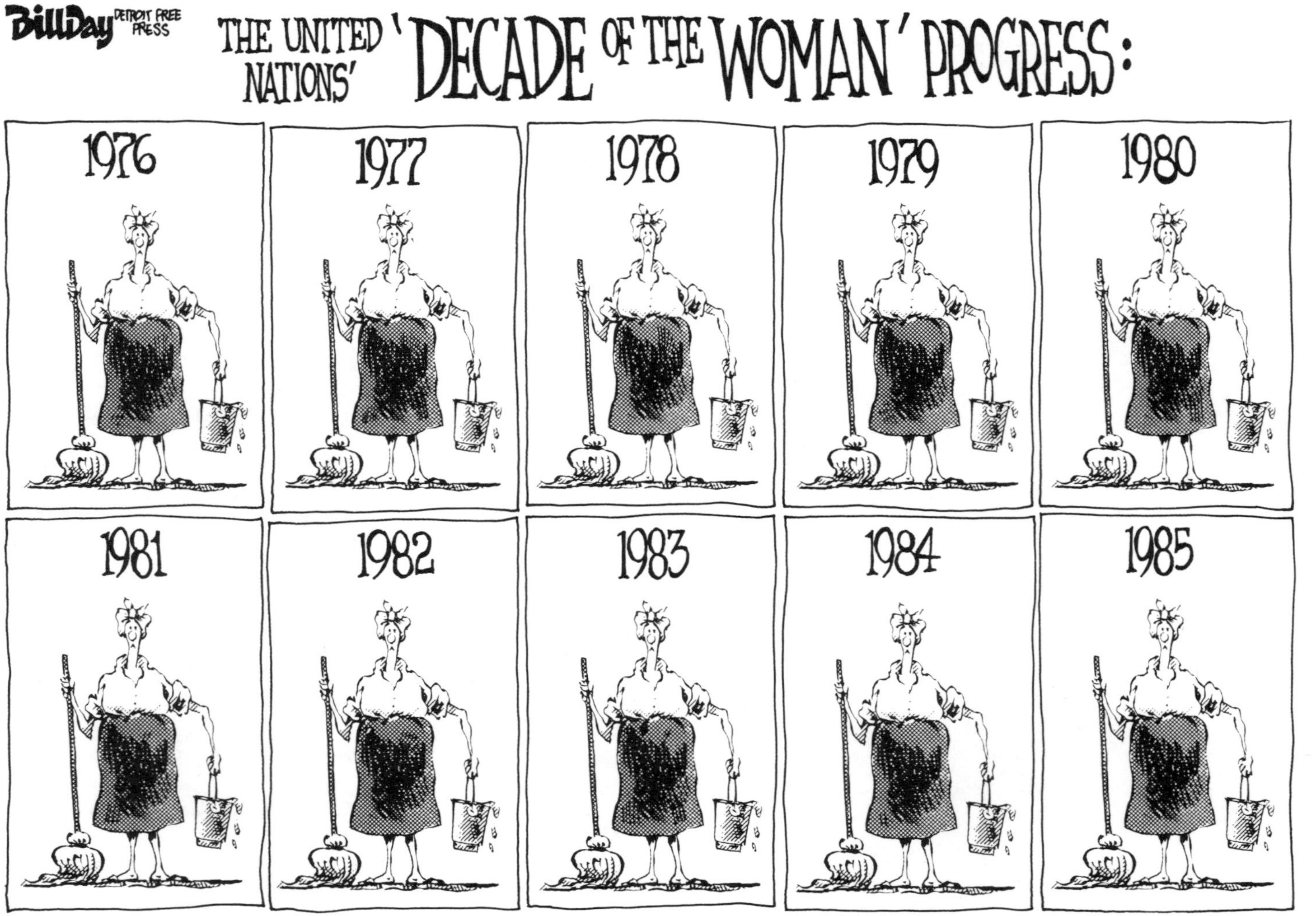
BillDay DETROIT FREE PRESS
THE UNITED NATIONS' 'DECADE OF THE WOMAN' PROGRESS:
1976
1977
1978
1979
1980
1981
1982
1983
1984
1985

June 26, 1985

WOMEN'S EQUALITY DAY - 1986

August 26, 1986

November 13, 1987

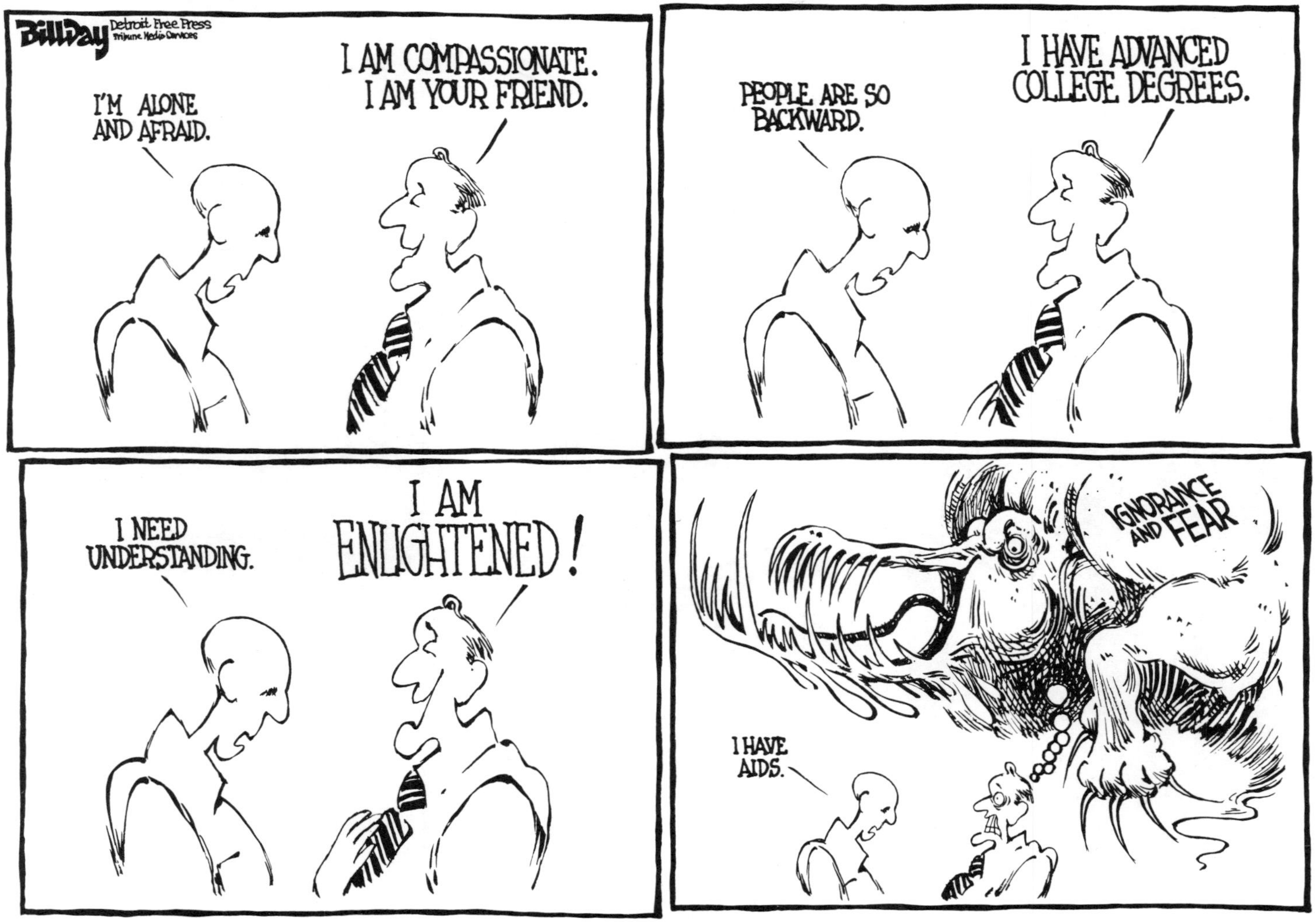
Bill Day
Detroit Free Press
Tribune Media Services
I'M ALONE AND AFRAID.
I AM COMPASSIONATE. I AM YOUR FRIEND.
PEOPLE ARE SO BACKWARD.
I HAVE ADVANCED COLLEGE DEGREES.
I NEED UNDERSTANDING.
I AM ENLIGHTENED!
IGNORANCE AND FEAR
I HAVE AIDS.

June 28, 1987

BILL DAY
Detroit Free Press
Tribune Media Services
BUT WAIT... WHAT IF HE ISN'T A PRINCE AND HASN'T PRACTICED SAFE SEX?!

June 11, 1987

BillDay
Detroit Free Press
Tribune Media Services
Our compassionate leader and keenest mind of the Free World, ignoring the technological resources of the most advanced medical and scientific community ever assembled on the face of the Earth, discovers on his very own the CURE for the deadly and heinous killer---AIDS.....
JUST SAY NO!

June 3, 1987

ALL THINGS RECONSIDERED

March 6, 1987

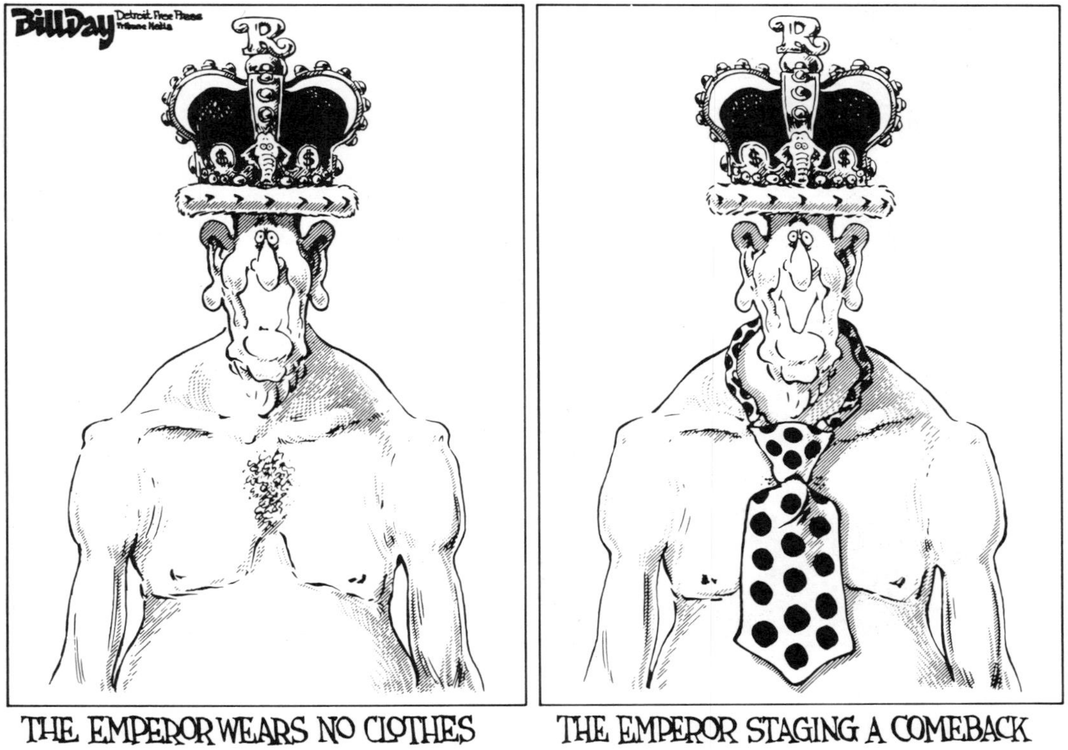

March 20, 1986

November 20, 1986

January 14, 1986

January 16, 1987

BillDay Detroit Free Press
Tribune Media Services
NEED A FAVOR?
"LEAVE IT TO DEAVER"

May 13, 1986

September 20, 1985

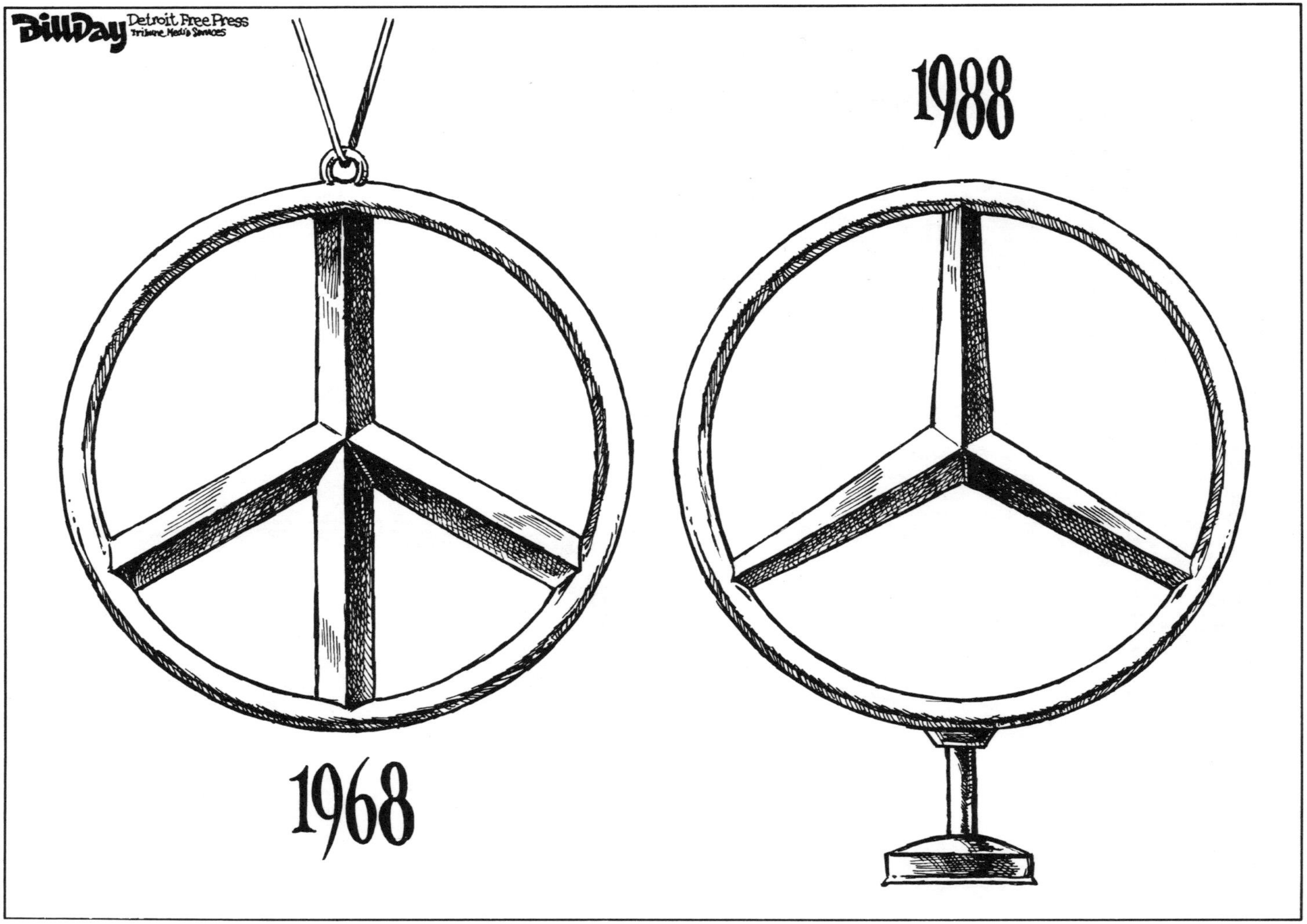

January 12, 1988

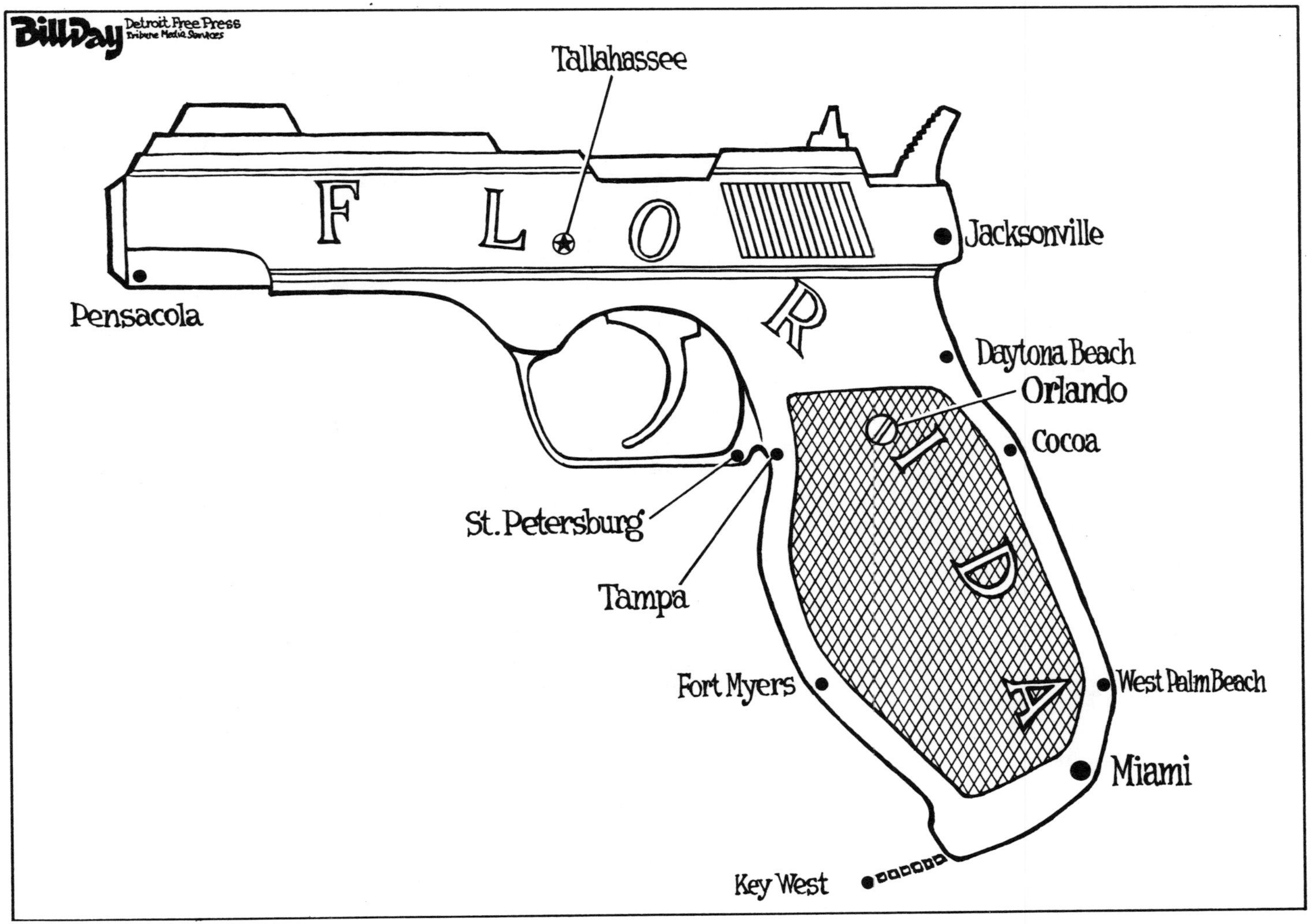

October 2, 1987

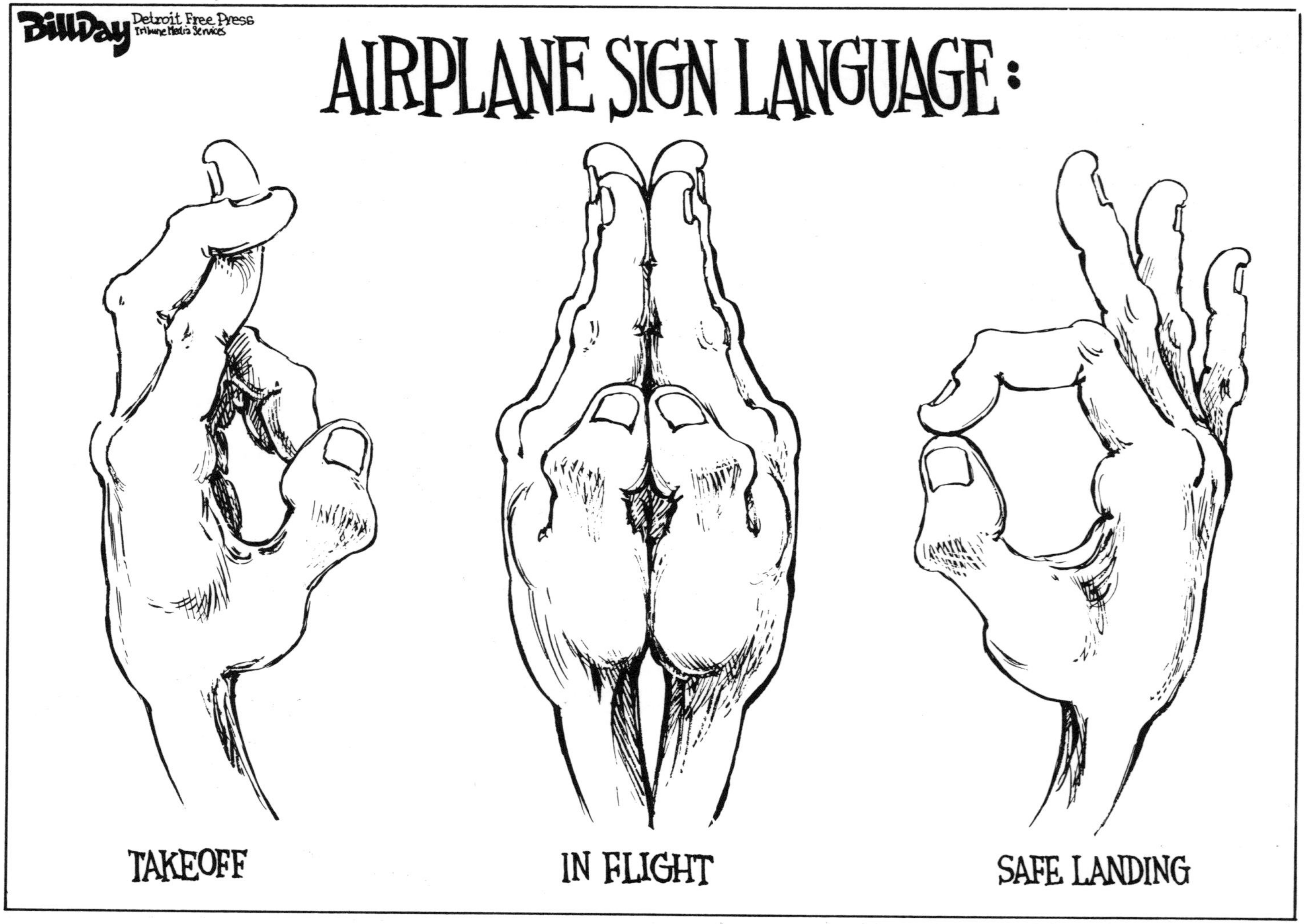

November 22, 1987

BillDay Detroit Free Press Tribune Media Services
DON'T BE SILLY, MILDRED... THERE'S NOT ANOTHER PLANE WITHIN A HUNDRED MILES OF US!!

July 15, 1987

November 12, 1987

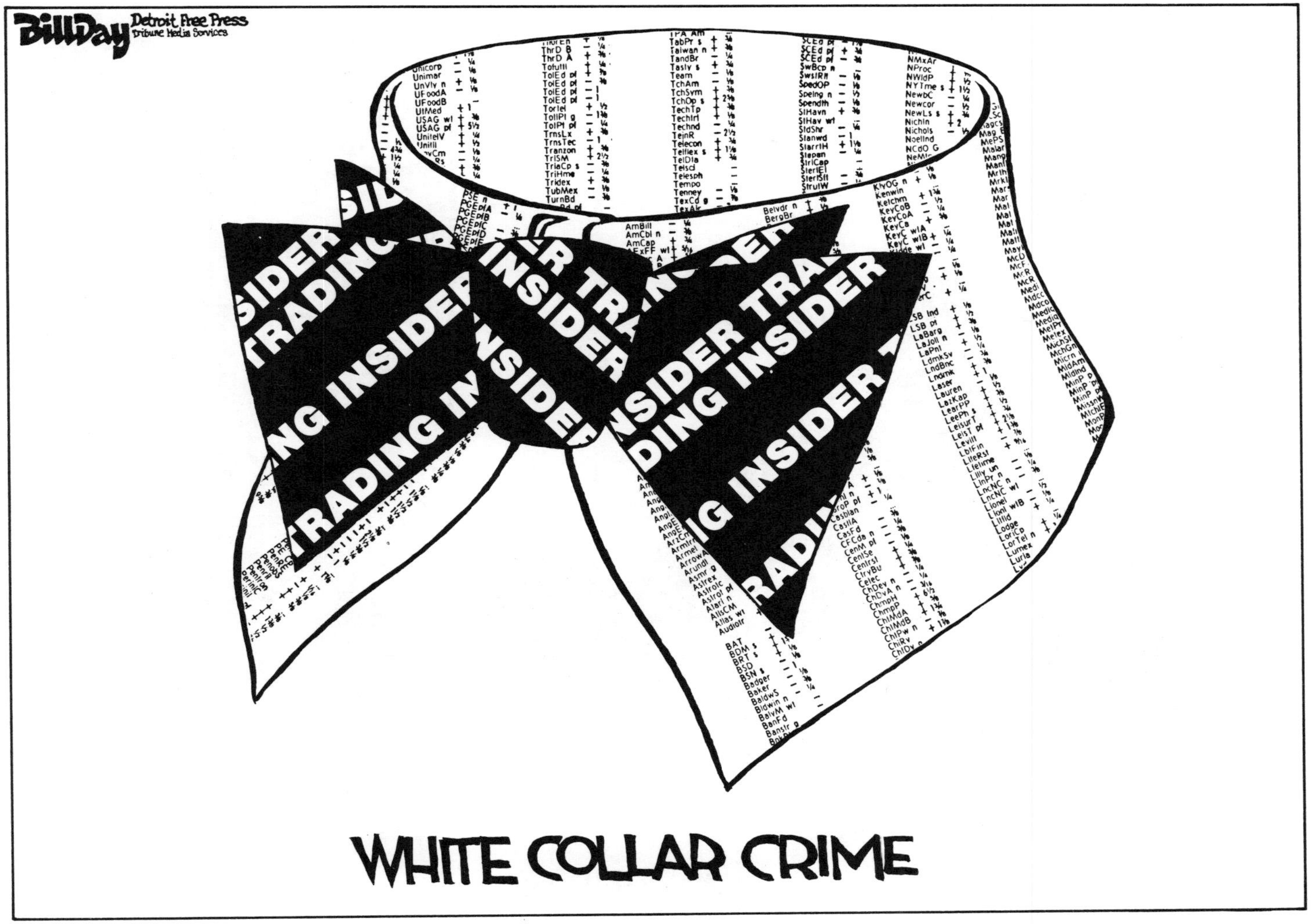

February 17, 1987

November 21, 1986

November 3, 1987

January 23, 1987

September 3, 1987

In Remembrance

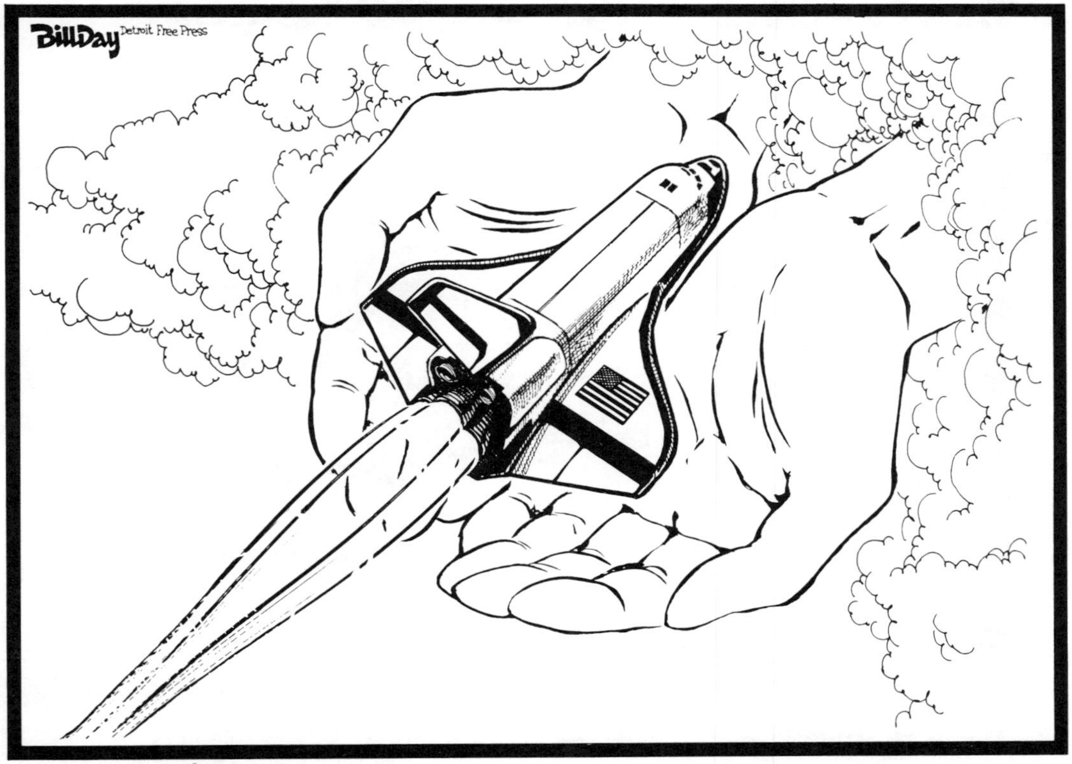

January 29, 1986

March 15, 1987

December 3, 1987

FRED ASTAIRE 1899-1987

June 24, 1987

BillDay Detroit Free Press Tribune Media Services
HOW SWEET IT IS!!

June 26, 1987

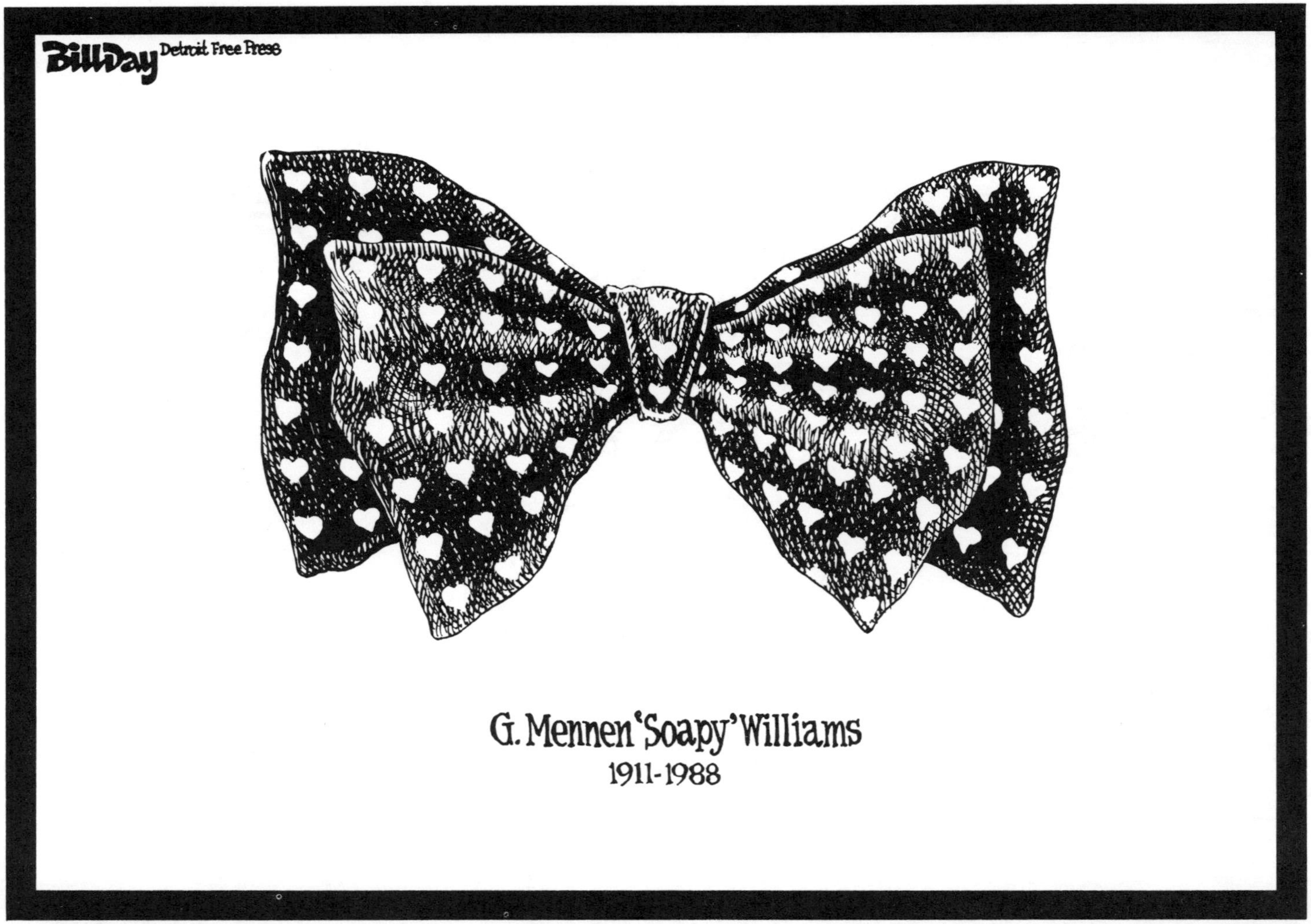

February 3, 1988

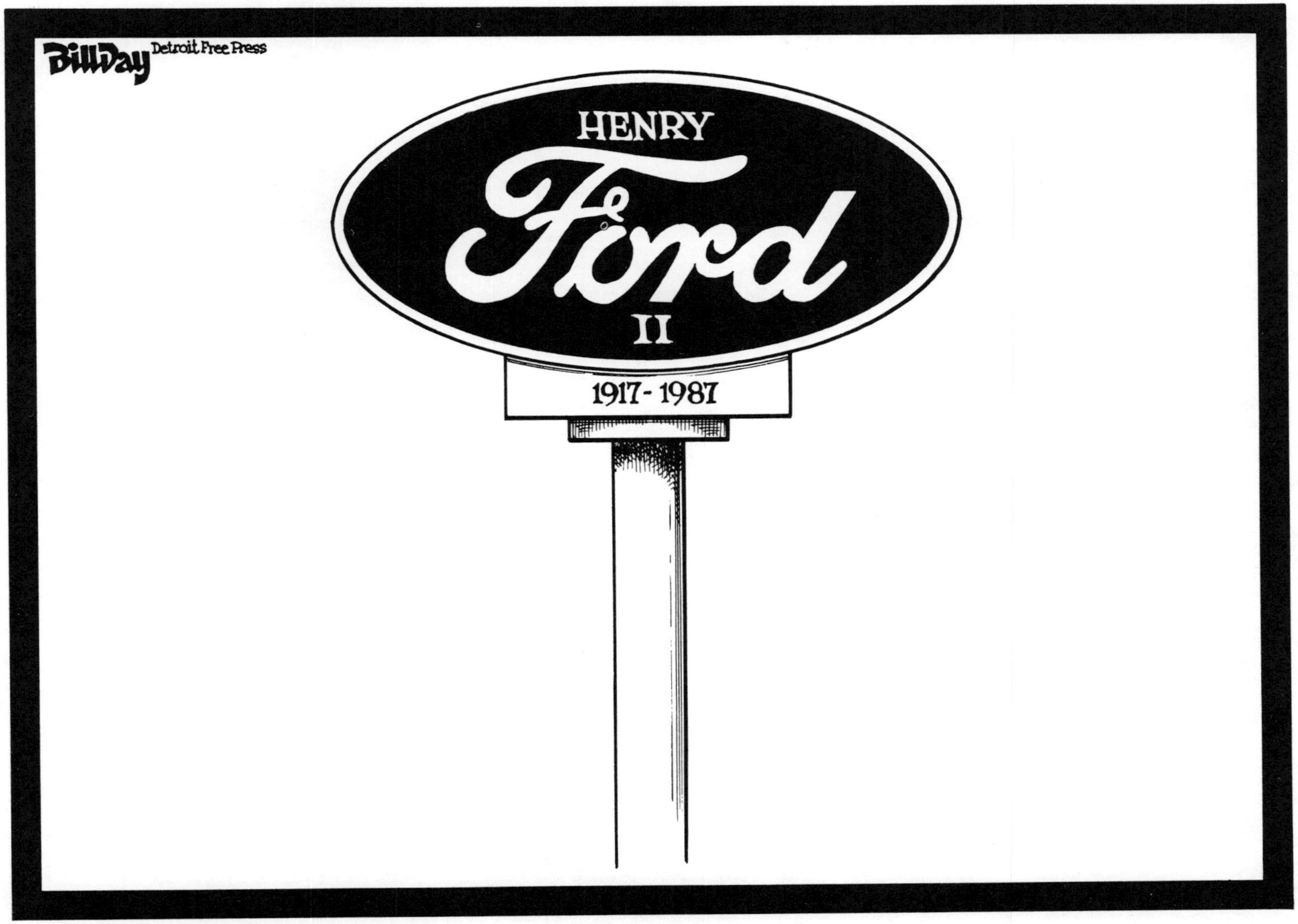

September 30, 1987

DETROIT: THE GOOD, THE BAD AND THE GUNS

August 21, 1986

August 6, 1987

December 9, 1986

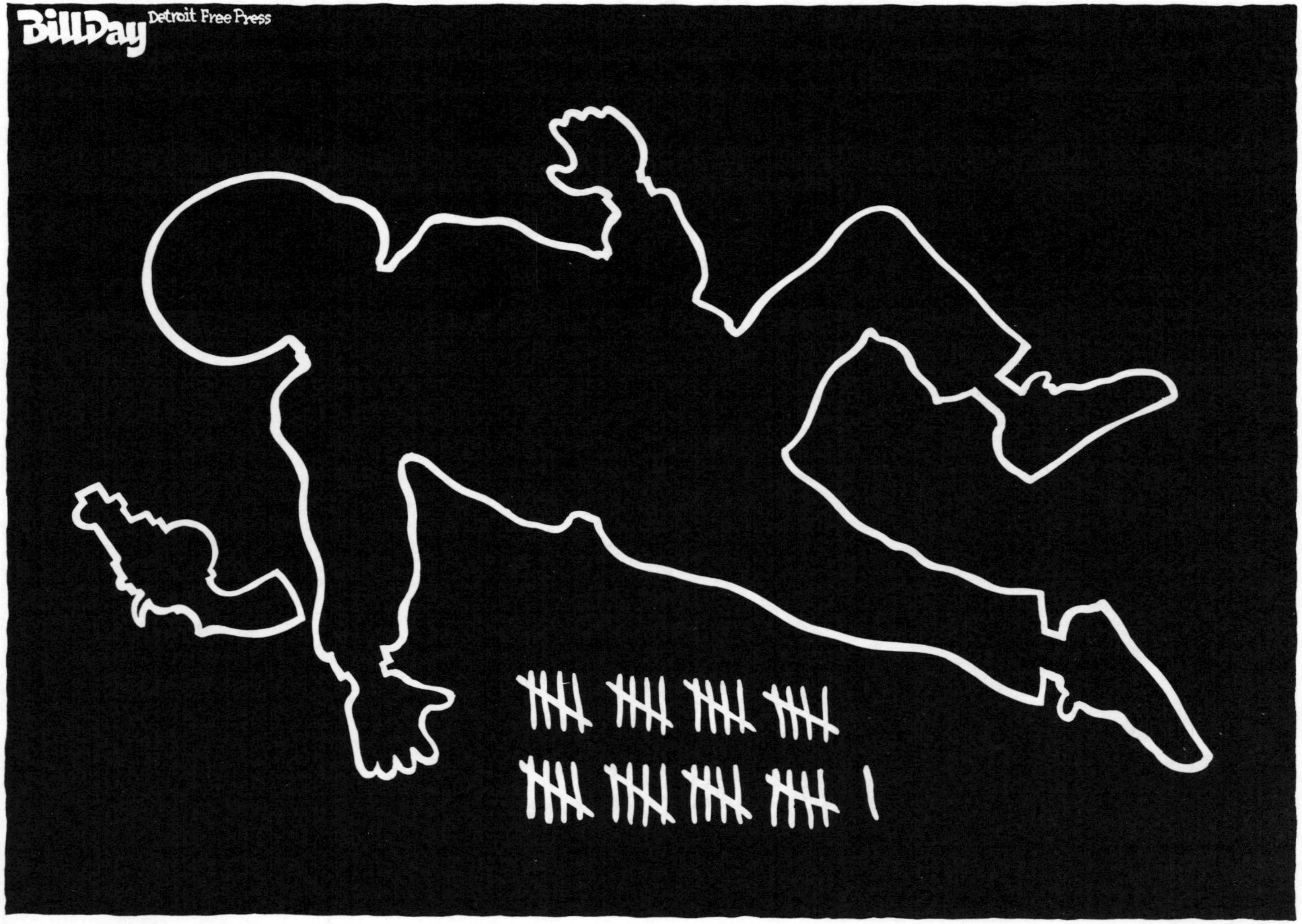

December 30, 1986

November 3, 1985

April 21, 1987

January 20, 1987

October 25, 1985

November 6, 1985

THE MAYOR AND HIS 'YES-MEN'

April 7, 1987

December 3, 1986

BillDay DETROIT FREE PRESS
PEOPLE MOVER PROBLEMS
SPIRIT OF TRANSPORTATION

May 3, 1985

BillDay
Detroit Free Press
ALL ABOARD!
Detroit
PEOPLE MOVER

June 26, 1987

July 15, 1988

April 11, 1985

November 12, 1986

November 9, 1986

December 3, 1986

The New Chrysler Symbol

April 16, 1985

March 19, 1987

October 13, 1985

April 14, 1985